About the Author

Born in Kentucky and now a dual Australian citizen living in Perth, Anil is a retired biologist, recently specialising in the use of word play around which to create literary and humorous writings. He has won awards for four of his earlier self-published books, some featuring animals and all involving some form of constrained writing around which are woven stories and essays, mostly silly nonsense. They are peppered with ongoing stories of his imaginary friends. As well as scientific papers Anil has contributed over two hundred articles to Word Ways; the Journal of Recreational Linguistics.

ABC# 101 Animal Universes

Anil

101 Animal Universes

Olympia Publishers
London

www.olympiapublishers.com
OLYMPIA PAPERBACK EDITION

Copyright © Anil 2023

The right of Anil to be identified as author of
this work has been asserted in accordance with sections 77 and 78
of the Copyright, Designs and Patents Act 1988.

All Rights Reserved

No reproduction, copy or transmission of this publication
may be made without written permission.
No paragraph of this publication may be reproduced,
copied or transmitted save with the written permission of the
publisher, or in accordance with the provisions
of the Copyright Act 1956 (as amended).

Any person who commits any unauthorised act in relation to
this publication may be liable to criminal
prosecution and civil claims for damage.

A CIP catalogue record for this title is
available from the British Library.

ISBN: 978-1-80074-734-0

This is a work of fiction.
Names, characters, places and incidents originate from the writer's
imagination. Any resemblance to actual persons, living or dead, is
purely coincidental.

First Published in 2023

Olympia Publishers
Tallis House
2 Tallis Street
London
EC4Y 0AB

Printed in Great Britain

Dedication

I dedicate this book to my recently deceased sister Sue Melton, who shared my sense of humour and inspired and often contributed to my writing. She will be sadly, badly missed.

Acknowledgements

Thanks to Sue, Dave Morice, Judith Bridges, and especially Jeff Grant for ideas and much invaluable feedback. Two rhymes were contributed by Jeff, both modified.

INTRODUCTION

These verses are monorhymes, written as a <u>constrained writing</u> challenge. My first poem as a youngster used this form:

> Walking down the street
> I met my pal Pete.
> We had a race and I beat.
> I said look at my feet,
>   they're so fleet.
> Now ain't that sweet.
>   (But not for Pete!)

Don't laugh, I was quite young. Teacher named it best in class! (Last line added later by Muse.)

This collection mixes fantasy, nonsense humour, sentimental poems, parody, satire and polemics, as the available pool of rhymes allowed. All to the beat of a rhythmic music of monometer monorhyme verses I call 'Uni-verses'. Universes are used in our two kids-of-all-ages books, *Silly Animal Rhymes and Stories A to Z* ['<u>SAR1</u>', 2018] and *SAR: Zoo Two* ['<u>SAR2</u>', 2021], both award winners. There they add prose story expansions and nonsense fantasy, nicely illustrated by award-winning Kalpart. Twenty-five of the 101 rhymes here are repeats from the *SAR* books minus the prose. The rest are new to books, but ten have been presented to Perth via WA Poets Inc, including four (22, 41, 54, 87) in their online poetry journal *Creatrix*, and three (13, 14, 16) have been published in the online hobby magazine, *Word Ways: Journal of Recreational Linguistics*.

> This is not a children's book. Several verses are too difficult for kids, a few too adult or gory. Parents might read most of the rhymes to kids, if requiring your help.

Some rhyming won't please everyone. Having lived under both US and Australian-British pronunciations I freely use either here. That's despite finding both groups mostly dismissive of or amused by (or ignorant of) the other's pronunciations.

Anil wanted to keep this a pure rhymes book, but Muse, the actual author, often added info notes, or one-line gags of the same ilk that more heavily infest much of the prose in the *SAR*s as well as in our recent award-winning etymology-based books of constrained writing, *Strange Bedfellows* (2019-20).

There are five chapters or groupings:

Dogs and Cats, Farm Animals, Primates, Wild, Mixed.

APOLOGIES

Sorry, no dalmatians. In this collection of light animal verse (occasionally heavy) I regret that 101 Dalmatians are not included, not even 001. Anticipating hostility, I tried for a rhyme with dalmatian but was overwhelmed. It has more rhymes than any other ending, way over a thousand! I couldn't cope with that much choice. I thought a simple parade to nowhere of animals that rhyme with dalmatians (Alsatians, cetaceans, crustaceans) was too pointless, and to probe into their procreations and mongrelisations too invasive.

Chapter 1. DOGS & CATS

1. RETRIEVER

Puppy Medicine

A pet retriever
to the true believer
and love receiver
is a great reliever.

2. BORZOI

Bad Puppy

My borzoi named Hoi Polloi
ate my koi like some sweet toy,
chewed up my best corduroy,
broke my antique Iroquois!

Gee, that pup can sure annoy,
ever likely to destroy!
Still, I call him 'Attaboy'
for he brings me so much joy.

3. POOCH

The next poem reports further mischief of Hoi.

Puppy Love on Grass

That frisky pooch
will chew on couch
then drink my hooch
and try to mooch
a slobbery smooch.
It makes me oooch!

4. HAIRLESS

Show Dog

This shaved-look mutt
named L'il Pee Nut
with stark haircut
and naked butt
looks like a slut
but sure can strut!

Poodle Noodle Soup

Does Putz Poodle
have a noodle
that can doodle?
Or's it futile?

She likes strudel!
Will that do till
I conclude all
this flapdoodle?

6. BLOODHOUND

Another Prisoner of the System
(unusual pure rhymes form restructured from SAR1)

Hound,
found downed,
Pound-bound,
frowned,
wound sound round ground.

7. PULI

Berserker

My pet puli
Mister Julie
saw a ghoulie!

Acted coolly?
No, the fool he
went unruly.

(...He said duly
to yours truly,
'You're a stoolie!')

8. DOG vs. CAT

Soggy Moggy

Little Moggy,
feeling groggy,
hit the bog. He
got all soggy.

'Waterloggy!'
laughed the doggy.

9. KITTEN

Kitty Ditty

Itty-bitty
little kitty
sure is pretty
but half-witty
at the city
nitty-gritty.

Poor lost kitty
doesn't fit! He
has my pity.

(Cat Committee
of the city
says 'Tough tittie.')

10. TOMCAT

Feline Terrorist

A cat, a tom,
set off a bomb
made of napalm
without a qualm.
'All for Islam!'

'Please to embalm
this mod phenom.
He's no Imam!'
says Muslim calm
Omar Khayyam.

Other Canines appear in chapter 4:
Coyote
and in chapter 5:
bulldog with **B**ullfrog
different **C**oyote et al.
dhole with **M**ole.
fox with **K**id
wolf with **D**odo.

Chapter 2. FARM ANIMALS

11. CHICKEN

Chickendom Patriotism

A witch, broom sticking,
made Chicken chicken
be panic-stricken
and (this will sicken)
run, lickey-splicking.
Said Chicken, clicking,
'A *true blue* Chicken,
I ain't fight picking!'

12. TURKEY

Christmas Leftovers (a whodunnit)

The turkey jerky
in Albuquerque
made us all perky,
each one a birkie.

Who killed the turkey
is still quite murky.
Is it Pa's work? He
does look smirky.

13. LAMB

Mary Had a Little Trouble

'Mare' (Mariam) had a little lamb?
No, 'twas a ram named Sleazy Sam!
They had a wham-bam-thank-you-Ma'am
and Sleazy Sam got Mare in jam.
He jumped a tram, went on the lam,
like in a scam the villain swam!

Then Mariam had little Mamb
(half-Mare, half-lamb),
part girl, part ram.
Mare did not scram to buy a pram.
Tell all? No, ma'am!
She played the clam.

To veil whim 'wham!' she hid young Mamb
with bold program of bald flim-flam.
Nor let it cram for school exam
for kids to slam and tease poor Mamb.
(Well I'll be damn! And what a sham(e).
She should have used a diaphragm!)

14. MULE

After Mary's little Mamb fled lockdown
Mary Had a Little Mule

For to give her life renewal
Mary got a little mule,
dyslexically coloured bule,
which she called her precious Jewel.

She once dragged the 'mule' to school,
which of course broke every rule.
Kids there laughed and called it fool,
teased it like some kind of ghoul.

Heated by this ridicule
mule got miffed and lost its cool,
kicked up in the vestibule,
broke kids' legs did reckless Jewel!

Cops agreed it wasn't cool,
threw Jewel in the swimming pool,
taught it how to toe the rule
and control that high joule fuel.

shock ending:
In shame Mary ate toadstool
with a poison molecule.
(Leaving lone poor orphan Jewel!
That, I think, was very cruel.)

But Is It Music?

Ms. Joan Red Roan,
whose beauty shone,
gave saxophone
a monotone
and boring drone.
It made me groan.

She needed shown.
I told fair Joan,
'Try xylophone
if music prone,
or leave alone.
The sax you've blown!'

16. DONKEY

Trick Question
(US usage)

Who said that lass
should rhyme with ass?
Some macho brass,
or wordsmith sass
just to harass
the female mass?
How very crass!

(No, no, the lass
young *jenny* ass
was meant to pass
this word test class.)

Other FARM animals appear in chapter 5:
chick with **T**ick
colt with **U**sain
duck with **J**ackal
ewe with **K**udu
goat with **C**oyote
goose with **M**oose
horse & foal with **V**ole & mole
Horse & zebra
Kid & squid etc.
pig with **E**arwig.

Chapter 3. PRIMATES

I confess, I'm a Primate Supremacist. They're my prime mates. Especially Bonobos [cf. SAR2]. Please support Friends of Bonobos orphan sanctuary and rehabilitation centre in DRCongo!

17. MONKEYS

Monkey Business

Punky Monkey,
music junkie,
played a plunky
banjo (one key)
he called Funky.

No one's flunky,
till his spunky
girlfriend monkey
Hunky Dunky
broke old Funky!

His world sunk. He
screamed she *stunk!*
He thus, poor Punky,
lost both Funky
and Miss Dunky.

18. POTTO

Gone to Potto

Dude lives in a grotto,
eats lots of risotto,
and drinks himself blotto.

He's hooked on the lotto.
'I'll win!' is the motto
of Otto the Potto.
— by Jeff Grant and Anil

19. ORANGUTANG [1] & SIAMANG

Two Nations Meet

Young red ape
Fang Orangutang
formed two-mates gang
with black ape
Twang Tang Siamang.

They shared ape slang
and proud songs sang.
From trees they swang,
played boomerang
without a prang.

They let it hang,
the whole shebang
like yin and yang,
nor gave a dang
from where they sprang.

---

[1] Orangutang, originally an ignorant spelling, is now acceptable. Ignorance rules!

20. ORANGUTAN

Racial Discrimination

The orangutan
has woods to span,
or zoos to scan
with cousins *Pan*.

He lives as can,
but must not fan
the Ku Klux Klan,
whose tirade ran:

'You're orange tan—
a *colored man!*
We must you ban—
or *harsher plan!*'

Monkey Murder

Uakari
was not chary
of that lorry.

Some safari
gang's shikari
made him quarry.

I'm so sorry.
Drink curare,
bad shikari[1]!

---

[1] The author does not condone capital punishment, merely reports what the rhymes dictate. I'm their boy. But the boy can't help wondering how many Incan(?) lives were lost during the centuries long process of discovering and developing the *use* of curare.

22. CAPUCHIN

Save the Monkeys!

The weeping ca*puch*in
of long evolution
might die of pollution!

No time for locution
nor hype diminution
for death's *no solution!*

Threatened Species

Lar the gibbon takes a whipping
from our human forest stripping,
our wood-chipping and off-ripping.
This, oh man, is so heart-gripping!

We're just stealing 'ownership'
in its home crib in one big gypping.
Let us do some big back-flipping
and a lot more fellowshipping!

24. YETI, the Abominable Snowperson

The Invention of Spelling

Sweaty Betty, clever yeti,
loved her alphabet spaghetti,
treating it just like confetti.

Then one day it spelt out YETI!
Now they call her Alpha Betty.

Other PRIMATES pop up in chapter 5:

Baboon, raccoon & loon
bonobo with **D**odo
chimpanzee with **S**ea Urchin
drill with **B**rill & krill
gorilla (silverback) with **Yak**
human with **Colt**
rock macaque with **Yak**.

Chapter 4. Other WILD ANIMALS

25. ALLIGATORS

Boy Meets Girl, Gator Style

'Al The Greater
Terminator'
met Girly Gator
at Beach Theatre.

Appreciate her?
Date her later?
Mate her?
Ate her!

26. ANTS

Ants in Pants
(US pronunciations)

Four ants in pants,
all four named Vance,
parade and prance
across green France
with cheerful chants
of ant romance.

Till their cute dance,
done to advance
their high finance,
ends by sheer chance
when they meet plants
who *swallow ants*[1]*!*

---

[1] I hope the pitcher plants choke on those pants! — and that the poet chokes on this repeat obsession with violence. *[Sorry, it gets worse.]*

27. ANTELOPE

An Optimist's Frustration

Ann Antelope
who's not a dope
can lope a slope
or walk tightrope.

Brain gyroscope
means she won't grope
so she says nope
to horoscope.

*But she can't cope
with you who mope
and lose all hope
like in a soap.*

28. BISON

Drug-Free!

Don't give bison streptomycin.
It's not nice and causes lysing!

29. BUNNY

Paradise Lost

'Bags' the Bunny,
bags of money,
private dunny,
thought life sunny—
till his Honey,
(dressed in gunny,
stockings runny)
stole his money.

'It's not funny!'
cried broke bunny[1].

---

[1] Punky Monkey would sympathise, even if you and I don't.

30. CATBIRD

What's in a Name?

The poor catbird
has never purred,
and isn't furred.
Its name's absurd!

And who conferred
on bird that word?
I haven't heard.
Some science nerd?

31. COD

A Fishmas Carol[1]

Part 1. Portrait
Ebenezer Cod
has turned from God
to give a nod
to get-rich plod.

This path he's trod
as mean tightwad
and boring clod
sans accolade.

Part 2. The Visitors
Tiny Tim Scrod
of damaged bod
and poorly shod,
plus ghosts (*no* bod)

---

[1] Plotline stolen from Charles Dickens, in case you thought it was original.

went to Eb Cod,
showed him his plod
was badly odd,
not worth its sod.

'Neath the facade
of being mod
you lack the od[1],
deserve the rod.'

Part 3. Denouement
Eb took the prod,
rejoined the squad,
gave love the nod
and shared his wad!

---

[1] Od is a mystical force behind everything, used here as the Fishmas spirit visited on Eb.

32. COYOTE #1 (coy-ot-ee)

Drug Dreams

Hippy Coyote
ate some peyote,
became a floaty
Don Quixote.

33. CROWS

Humans Not Needed

The much cursed crows
did not wear clothes
nor house repose
e'en after snows,
yet never froze
their beaks or nose
nor e'en their toes!

*(Do you suppose
they wore warm hose?)*

34. CRANE

My Fair Crane

The crane in Spain
stays mainly on the plain.
Through snow and rain
and heat insane
Sis won't complain.

Her main campaign?
Replace plain grain
(and hunger pain?)
with sugar cane,
perhaps chow mein!

…It's all in vain.
So poor Sis Crane
must yet maintain
again and again
on plain plain grain.

35. DARTER

Not Political, Thanks

Dash Darter a martyr
for President Carter?
No way, he was smarter—
a quick scene departer!

(And hence the name *darter*?)

36. DRUM FISH

A Friend Twice Over

'Hum' Drum is no bum
tho he come from the scum.

Hum makes a great chum
for when you feel glum.

Then, cooked with some plum,
your dinner—yum-yum[1]!

---

[1] Does everybody eat their friends, Anil wonders? And pardon if I point out a couple of puns here. **Chum** is slang for fish chopped for bait, *and* chum is a species of fish (unrelated to drum). The sufficiently ignorant might think it means drumfish, okay?

37. ELEPHANT

Funny, He Didn't Notice

The elephant in the room[1]
was unspotted by the zoom
of a daydreaming young groom
as his wedding hour did loom.

'If it doesn't wear perfume
or not shock me with a boom
or not threaten me with doom
I will sweep it as I broom.'

---

[1] Whence the Elephant, you ask? A wedding gift of course. Elephants are a common wedding gift among the upper classes in India and Thailand.

Nazi Racism

'Extermine
non-German
born ermine
—they're *vermin!*
said Hermann
G's sermon.

A Little Bird Told Him (Off)

Brother Flicker,
known nit-picker,
loves to bicker.
Sees the vicar
steal some liquor
with a snicker.

Outraged flicker
tells the vicar,
'Nasty liquor!
Nothing's slicker
than that tricker
You should kick 'er!'

Foxy Lady

You should see young Fanny Fox,
hip freak from the far boondocks
wearing Rastaman dreadlocks!

I know it's not orthodox
—but some say a paradox
coming from Pandora's box!

Well, I wish on them a pox,
them she easy could outfox.
They've dementia praecox!

41. GAUR

Flower Power

Do not cower at the gaur
named Dwight David Eisenhower
though he glower and look sour.

Give a flower! Watch him shower
you with power by the hour,
not devour your home bower.

42. GNOME

Gnome Control

If ever a gnome
should visit your home
don't spray it with foam
nor seek help from Rome,
just tell it 'Shalom!'

Then read it a poem
or long palindrome
and watch it go roam
back into the loam,
its underground home[1].

---

[1] Gnomes allegedly guard earth's treasures. They've surely let us down lately! When a Gnome next visits your home ask it what happened. *Then tell the world!*

43. GOPHER

Spoilt Rich Lady

Jo 'Fur' Gopher
is a loafer.
She has dough fer
ten times over
cost of chauffeur
and a gofer.

She has shopping sprees in Ophir,
pays much mo' for
toy boy Oaf, her.

Exercise? She 'pounds' the sofa.
And if angry pounds Oaf gopher.

Omnivore

Swami Gourami
ate some pastrami
then chopped tatami
and then his mommy.

45. GUINEA PIG

Don't Rock the Ship!

The Cavy Navy
gets wavy gravy.

Shark Warning!

Don't get chummy
with a gummy,
silly dummy!

You'll look yummy
and be scrummy
in its tummy!

47. HADDOCK

Know Your Place!

Once a nut case haddock
by the name of Braddock,
when he felt nomadic
made a leap sporadic
to an empty paddock[1].

As a water addict
I'm afraid he's had it.

---

[1] In *SAR2* a whale made a similar rash and foolish leap. One case is strange enuf but two is verging on the supernatural.

48. LOCUSTS

Insects of Disaster

A swarm of locusts
with quite clear focus
and hocus -pocus
ate all our crocus
and crops! It woke us—
and truly broke us.
And that's not joke-ous[1]!

---

[1] No, definitely no humour here. It's one of God's ways of telling us there's more of us than He planned on. Some say He planted covid-19 in order to top trim the human tree, hoping to lop 5% of us in a Universe instant. Help, what next?

    It's understandable actually. God needs to lighten His load in order to be able to handle the excess population. It's really hard to keep up with all the attention each person demands of Him, not to mention the paperwork—near eight billion alive, over one hundred billion dead and ? billions to come! Not to mention billions of other Creations in our Universe. And countless other Universes? It gives Him a headache. Imagine the cross referencing required. Many a googolplex of connections and groupings and all the future lines of possibility.

    He can have it. I wouldn't accept Godhood if offered.

49. MOTH

Clergymen Copy Insects

The baby moth
is strangely loth
to feast on broth.

Priests too would froth.
It seems they both
prefer the cloth.

Amphibian? FISH!

Meet young Flipper,
 cute mudskipper,
 heartstrings gripper.

  Double dipper,
  she's both ripper
   water slipper ~~~~~~~
   and a chipper
   skinny-dipper
   sunshine tripper. ⎯⎯⎯⎯⎯⎯

51a. NEMATODE

A Gory Ode

Nem Nematode[1]
of man abode,
when life's hard road
and heavy load
made him feel mowed,
that he was owed,
chose to explode.
Blood and guts flowed.

(That's worth an ode??)

---

[1] There's another, happier Nematode story next.

Tode of Toad Hall
(A Pet Roundworm)

Was Nee Ma Tode
of guts abode
inside Todd Toad
a great big load?

Was old toad slowed?
Or buffaloed?
Did Tode make Toad
swell up? Explode?

No, Tode just glowed
and overflowed.
Hence toad bestowed
on Tode this ode[1].

---

[1] If only Nem, the tragic human Nematode in 50a, had had a friendly host like Todd!

52. OCELOT

52a. Mixed Signals

Most ocelot
I fathom not,
with stripe *and* spot
(line, polka dot)
like some weird blot
in crazy knot.

52b. Nature's Way

The ocelot
has got a plot,
like it or not,
to toss your tot
in boiling pot
and eat it hot!

Should it be shot
and left to rot?
No, Nature's not
always a trot
to some jackpot
for us men, what?

53. OWL

Beware the Owl!

The killer Al Owl
is such a foul fowl!

When Al's on the prowl
he hoots with a howl
that's more like a growl,
and has such a scowl
he'll cause you to yowl
and may move your bowel!

(So carry a towel.
Or maybe a trowel!)

54. PLAICE

Plaice's Face Changes Place!
(an action thriller)

The plaice fish race
enjoy slow pace
and mostly stay in just one place.

Except the face
(a sad disgrace)
which moves *across* the small braincase!

55. PLOVER

Just a-Looking for a Home[1]
(translation of a bird song)

I, Lonely Pal Plover,
do seek to uncover
a place I can hover
and welcome a lover
to cuddle and smother.

Or maybe a brother,
or even a mother.
One or the other!

---

[1] See Weevil for the original singer of the title folk song. Whether Lonely Pal ever realised his dream must remain undisclosed in order to maintain the pathos.

56. TAPIR

Another Tragic Toilet Paper Shortage

Farty Tapir
had no paper
so his caper
left a vapour—
'No Escaper!'

Also available as a Limerick.

The rude Fartee Tapir
had no toilet paper
so her homer
left 'a roamer'.
No one could escape her!

57. TARDIGRADE (WATER BEAR)

Renegade Tardigrade Escapade

1.
Wee Tardigrade,
a moss bear maid
once had it made
in old decade
like 'in the shade',
was very staid,
nor e'er afraid.

2.
Till a home raid
and way blockade
she can't evade
had her waylaid:
The Tax Brigade
came to degrade
for fine unpaid.

3.
The story weighed
saw justice fade.
A big parade
and cavalcade,
soon a cascade
formed a Crusade,
came to Wee's aid

4.
Their charges laid
severe upbraid
on the Brigade.
'It's a charade,
their case cliched,
a masquerade
we once forbade[1]!'

---

[1] Anil's friend Judge Gduj ruled that, as a homeless microscopic creature, Wee owed only a microscopic amount of tax, far less than 1¢, hence uncollectible. The tax people as usual were just greedily trying to tax everyone and everything in sight.

58. TENREC

The Taming of the Shrew by a Shrew

Toulouse-Lautrec,
who's no roughneck,
used his tenrec
to hold in check
his wife's henpeck.

59. THROSTLE (SONG THRUSH)

Bumptious Pretender
(US pronunciations)

Throb the Throstle,
self-colossal
fake Apostle[1],
loves to jostle,
won't be docile
till a fossil!

---

[1] Throb Throstle imagines he's a rebirth of St. John entitled to bump into others boldly without apology. Was St. John really like that?

60. TROUT

Climate Change

Now that the drought
affects Ted Trout
I hear him pout
and loudly shout,
'My water spout
has ceased to sprout!
What's it about?'

*(Sorry, devout,
please don't me flout.
I lack the clout
to help Ted out.)* [1]

---

[1] I lied here for the sake of a resonant closing verse. I *do*, as part of the body politic, have the clout to do something about climate change. We all do and must.

61. WEEVIL

Name Calling

He may be primeval
but beetle Boll Weevil
can cause an upheaval
that's way past retrieval.

And *he's* past reprieval,
so we name him Evil.[1]

---

[1] Like locusts, another unloved marvel of Nature.

62. WILDEBEEST

Gnus in Shoes

Smart gnus in shoes
don't board canoes.
With poke-me-throughs
as sharp as screws
it makes them ooze
(that is, canoes),
which gives them blues
(that is, *dumb* gnus).

63. XIPHIAS

Swordfish Rave

All hail Zip Xiphias,
the ocean's jiffiest!
Though some say iffiest,
I say the spiffiest!

Other WILD ANIMALS appear in chapter 5.
addax, diamondback, hyrax, muntjacs with **Y**aks
barn owl with **C**ooter
bee with **F**lea and with **S**ea Urchin
bobolink and mink with **S**kink
cassowary with **C**anary
chiton with **T**riton / chough with **R**uff
chuckwalla with **I**mpala
drill, krill, whippoorwill with **B**rill
duck, loon, raccoon with **B**aboon
fantail, quail and snail with **Z**iphius
flea with **S**ea Urchin / grackle with **J**ackal
jerboa and protozoa with **M**oa
John Dory with **L**ory
kangaroo with **K**udu
katydid and squid with **K**id
Komodo dragon with **D**odo
louse with **N**udibranch
mole, tadpole, sole, oriole, redpoll, frog, troll, fox w/ **V**ole
peacock with **S**pringbok
pigeon with **W**igeon,
quail and nightingale with **W**agtail
rail with **Q**uail and with **W**agtail
roc with **C**roc
rook and snook with **G**erenuk
shearwater with **O**tter
stoat with **C**oyote
weaver with **B**eaver
whale (Baleen) with **S**ardine
zander with **C**ondor
zebra with **H**orse

Chapter 5. MIXED SPECIES

64. BABOON, RACCOON & LOON

Dream Bully

A sick cartoon
shows Cheer Raccoon
and Claire the Loon
in thought balloon
of Badd Baboon.

A monkey goon
and big buffoon,
he'd cook them soon
with macaroon
and eat by spoon.

He'd change his tune
if Badd knew loon
mixed with raccoon
would make him swoon
and turn maroon!

— by Dr. Duck, guest poet[1]

---

[1] You must trust my prognosis here until it's disproved in the lab. – Dr. Duck

65. BEAVER & WEAVER

Builder vs. Builder

The weaver, to peeve her,
in jibe said that beaver's
an underachiever.

'Underwater heaver!'
replied the hurt beaver.
'Water's a deceiver,
you first-look believer
and bad misconceiver.
A first grade school leaver?

'Still, I won't play griever
with vengeance born fever
and hack you with cleaver.'[1]

---

[1] Ms. Beaver's restraint paid off. They became friends afterwards.

66. BRILL, KRILL, WHIPPOORWILL, DRILL

RHYMING ILL-DICTATES DIET.
(in 3 parts)

Part 1. Narrow Diets

a. Bill Brill eats krill
   against his will,
   but eats them still.
   They make him ill.
   He's kind of sill.

b. Kurt Krill eats spill
   of fish from kill,
   as suits his will.
   (If fish is Bill
   it's *self-fullfill!*)

Part 2. Broad Diet

Sue Whippoorwill
atop the hill
starts out with dill
for chlorophyll
then daffodil
to add a frill,
then raids the mill
to fill her bill.

Part 3. No Diet

Watch Jill the Drill
instil goodwill!

That is until
she craves a meal.
Then, so unreal,
she dreams of brill
hot off the grill,
baked whippoorwill
mixed in with swill,
and side dish krill.
But she has nil.

Poor hungry Jill
of once good will
cries out so shrill
we'll rob the till
to keep her still.

67. BULLFROG & BULLDOG

Fair Trade?

Bullfrog ate a small hot dog.
Bulldog ate a small hot frog.
Such equality to log
left me totally agog.
(And an orphan pollywog.)[1]

---

[1] Thankfully Po Orphan tadpole was adopted by Vole and Mole in #97 and shined.

68. CANARY & CASSOWARY

Beauty and the Beast

<u>JANUARY</u>:
Sue Canary's
very wary
of big hairy,
extra-scary
cassowary!

<u>FEBRUARY</u>:
Visionary,
Sue Canary
chose to *bury*
'Bestiary'
dictionary.

<u>MARCH</u>: Her very
imaginary
adversary,
solitary
cassowary,
Sue did marry!

69. COLT & HUMAN

Fastest Man Alive!

Super-speedy Usain Bolt
tried to chase a free wild colt.
Catch it?
No, you silly dolt.

70. COOTER & OWL

Anti-Gun Lobbyists

Tugg Turtle, a cooter,
and Barn Owl, a hooter,
share-ride on a scooter.

They don't need a tutor
or Apple computer
to spot Ann Sharpshooter.

'She's just a freebooter,
a mean wildlife looter.
They should execute her!'[1]

---

[1] The author does not condone this solution. See disclaimer in #21.

71. CONDOR & ZANDER

ANIMAL SCIENTISTS?

Bird Astronomer?

Does the condor
ever ponder
what's up yonder?
Or just maunder
and so squander
its sky wander?

Fish Oceanographer?

Does the zander [1]
ever ponder
what's down yonder?
Or just maunder
and so squander
its deep wander?

---

[1] Compare Zander and Salamander in SAR2 for the preferred pronunciation of zander.

72. COYOTE #2 (ki-oat),[1] GOAT & STOAT

Coyote Tells a Story

Mean Kai Coyote
bit poor Zy Goat
right thru the throat
  just for to gloat,
  then left a note
  and hid! I quote:

'Tain't I that smote
this here dead goat.
I was remote.
The cutthroat stoat [2]
did in the goat.'
(His lie won't float!)

---

[1] See #31 for the alternative pronunciation, coy-o-tee.
[2] The Stoat wasn't even there but had gone home to the United Stoats of Armenia.

73. CROCODILE & ROC

Violent Roc Croc Attack
[Skip this one if you're squeamish.]

When Jock the Croc
saw Giant Roc
wearing a smock
he just to mock
the Roc's smart frock
and for to shock
gave him a knock.

G. Roc, proud cock,
then went amok,
picked up the croc
in tight headlock
and flung it *(sock!)*
against a rock.
This ruined Jock.[1]

---

[1] There is no moral here. This was too long ago to have a moral.

74. DODO et al.

Whodunit?[1]

Who killed dodo?
Was it Frodo?
The Komodo?
The bonobo?
The wolf lobo?
Or a solo
drop-out hobo
who went loco?

'No!' says Pogo,
''twas our dough-go!
Every Joe Blow,
you and me, Bro,
brought the woe throw,
the big low mow
and the death blow.'

What a no-no!
Woe on us schmo.
Like a yoyo
we'll join dodo.

---

[1] This tense murder mystery/polemic isn't a pure universe. It mixes pseudo-rhymes.

75. EARWIG & PIG

Giant Insect Story
(non-horror)

Big Earl Earwig
met cute Miss Pig
at cool shindig.

They had a swig
and did a jig
and both fell big.

Now she's Pig-Wig
and he's Ear-Pig
and they've offsprig!

76. FLEA & BEE

Tea Party[1]
Freddie FLEA, Florence BEE
having tea in this tree
is so
twee
I must
flee
lest
I pee
upon me!

---

[1] This word drawing of a tea party in a tree is a caricature. In real life the two insects aren't that big.

77. GERENOOK, SNOOK & ROOK

A Soft-Headed Softy

Gert Gerenuk
caught Sally Snook
with fishing hook
in her salt brook.

Sal cried 'I'm took!'
Gert's mind then shook.
'I'm no fish crook!'
she said to Rook.

So she forsook
her plan to cook
the helpless snook
and ate the rook.

78. HORSE & ZEBRA

78a.
Watch What You Say, Charley!

Old Charley Horse
wrote a discourse
tapped out in Morse,
some words quite coarse!
He begged the Force
at his racecourse not to divorce
him but endorse.
'You a resource?'
They mock remorse,
say 'Tough darts, horse!',
sign intercourse.

78b.
Horse of a Different Stripe

Debra Zebra[1] was a 'horse',
a true term I can endorse.
She had stripes as well of course.
Deb was Charley's romance source,
drawn by a magnetic force!

---

[1] I promised the kids in SAR2 I'd write a Debra Zebra rhyme. But will they ever see it hidden away in an adult book? Maybe after they grow up? Or could you tell them?

79. IMPALA & CHUCKWALLA

Unappreciated Gift from Above

To the starved impala
the immense chuckwalla
was a gift from Allah
that he could not swallow.

80. JACKAL, DUCK, GRACKLE

Jack's Shack

Jack the Jackal
makes me cackle,
nor'd he ever raise a hackle.

But his home is some debacle,
a ram-shackle
Help can't tackle.

Dr. Duck the well-known quack'll
help unshackle
jackal's shack,
all subcontracted to a grackle
high on drug of Dr. Jekyll!

81. KID, SQUID, KATYDID & FOX SID

81a.
A Nature Lover

Nicole the Kid
e'er hid her id
amid the squid
and katydid.

81b.
…And Her Unnatural End

She had a skid
in old Madrid.
Her debt to rid
she made a bid,
ten thousand quid,
on pyramid
with bookie Sid.[1]
(Oh, God forbid!)

---

[1] I hope Sid got did. Voluntary manslaughter!

When she got did
she blew her lid
and poor Nic slid
right off the grid.

82. KUDU, EWE, KANGAROO

Toilet Debate[1]

'How do you do?'
I ask a few
at City Zoo,
like kudu, ewe
and kangaroo.

They misconstrue:
'We don't doo, Hugh,
We use voodoo,
and you we boo!
How do *you* doo?'

'I use a loo,
and you should too!
But you just pooh
at will and shoo.
That's rude & blue.

(But, to speak true,
I envy you!)'

---

[1] This builds on a rhyme in SAR1 (Kangaroo).

83. LORY & JOHN DORY

A Lory-Dory Allegory

The lovebird lory
did peck John Dory.
'Twas amatory
not predatory.

But it was gory
and without glory.
It sent the dory
to crematory!

Moral of story?
An allegory:
What's good for lory
ain't hunky-dory!

84. MOA, PROTOZOA, JERBOA & HORDES

Double Extinction Story

Noah said Hello Aloha
to the desert rat jerboa
and a *horde* of metazoa

but a sad Goodbye Aloha
to the giant flightless moa
and the moa's protozoa,

stuck Down Under, a no-shower
at the ark of saviour Noah—
couldn't make it in their proa![1]

---

[1] There weren't many flights between New Zealand and the Holy Land back then. And their South Pacific sailing canoe (proa) was too slow to make the 'deadline'.

85. MOLE & DHOLE

Noel Mole Learns Too Late[1]

This lazy mole
without a goal
let ethanol
come take its toll.

To fill the hole
Noel went and stole
a jellyroll
from someone's bowl.

Guess who's—Dan Dhole!
Dan lost control
and ate Noel whole.[2]
(Well bless my soul!)

---

[1] FYI, Noel Mole is not related to Moe Mole, whom we'll meet under **V**ole (#97). Ironically, not Moe but his burrow-mate Voe Vole also turned to thieving. Oops, I've stolen the punch of #97. However, it's far enough away you should have plenty of time to forget it and be surprised.

[2] Dan's short temper reminds us of Giant Roc (#73).

86. MOOSE & GOOSE

Bruce and Seuss

A moose named Bruce
struck mad by Zeus
played loose with Seuss,
a spruce young goose.

Now what the deuce?
Abuse? No, *juice!*
— by Jeff Grant and Anil

87. NUDIBRANCH & LOUSE

Pushy Banks Branch Out

Nell Nudibranch
first drew a blank
when asked which bank
she'd like to thank
by Nit, rep for a US bank.

She said 'I thank
The Nudi Bank
as I'm myself a -Branch of rank.
Its honest plank
has lots of swank.'

Nit got quite rank,
and rude and frank
he said point blank
her Nude Bank stank,
and they'd outflank
it so it sank.

Nell said 'Go wank,
you fucking Yank!'[1]

---

[1] I tried to get Nell to tone down her language, but she was quite agitated.

88. OTTER & SHEARWATER Daughter

Otter Mischief

A police blotter
says: 'Hairy Potter,
the young girl otter,
tho a globetrotter
is a real rotter
and mischief plotter:

'She with a swatter
caused Ms. Shearwater's
young trusting daughter
to teeter totter
into the water.
She shouldna oughter!'

89. QUAIL & RAIL

Quail Grail Quest

A questing quail
thought he could trail
the Wizard Rail
and so unveil
the Holy Grail.

But Wizard Rail
drank too much ale
and went to jail!
Thus ends in fail
this almost tale.

90. RUFF & CHOUGH

Close Encounters of the Birdkind

Rolf Ruff did huff
in voice right gruff
and act real tough
to Charlie Chough.
'I you will snuff
for your rebuff!'

(It's all just bluff.
Not tough enough
to scare Chas. Chough.
Rolf's mostly fluff
and softer stuff,
a powder puff.)

91. SARDINE & BALEEN WHALE

Ocean Potatoes

Old Salt Sardine
and Whale Baleen
watched shows all keen
on wet-proof screen
on submarine-
type film machine
from scene to scene
to scene to scene
to scene to scene…

Ain't since been seen.

92. SEA URCHIN, BEE, CHIMPANZEE, FLEA

The Sting

The urchins of sea
can sting like a bee.

'Well, I stay sting-free,'
said Chip Chimpanzee.
'They never Chip see
cause water scares me.'

Then (ha! iro*ny!*)
Chip's bit by a flea!

93. SKINK, BOBOLINK & MINK

The Skink in Pink

'Slink Skink, I think,
looks dink in pink.'
said bobolink
to sourpuss mink.

'If you don't wink
and we don't link,
you stink, you fink,
you useless mink!'

94. SPRINGBOK & PEACOCK

Classical Music Rebels

Why'd Springbok Jacques
and Peacock Ok
dare shock the flock
to play hard rock?

'Coz Bach, Bartok,
gay Offenbach
and old Dvorak
are such a crock!'

95. TICK & CHICK

Sadist Tick

The tick on the chick
can lick it and prick
and quick make it sick.

The chick cannot trick
nor flick the bad tick.
It really can stick.

This thick-as-a-brick
mean tick gets a *kick*
from pricking the chick!

96. TRITON and CHITON

Mollusks Will Be Mollusks

Triton, chiton,
always fightin'!
Not to frighten,
nor enlighten.
Just delight in
fun of fightin'.
'So excitin'!'

97. VOLE, MOLE, TADPOLE, Onlookers & FOX

A NOVELISSIMOLE (in 3 voles)

vole 1.

Vole and Mole Raise a Frog

Voe the Vole and Moe the Mole
shared a home, a cubbyhole
in the north side of a knoll.

Both of them were on the dole
and they had no lifetime goal,
hence no boring rigmarole.

Yet folks loved cute Po Tadpole [1]
Orphan in their goldfish bowl,
drinking to it, saying skol!

Fish compared it to a sole.
Birds said no, an oriole!
Or perhaps a bright redpoll.

Horses loved it like a foal.
Frogs declared it very droll.
It even amused a Troll!

vole 2.
Voe Vole Breaks Bad

This was all till Voe the Vole
went bad weird and upped and stole
poor blind Woe Worm's payroll whole.

Soon the smart earthworm patrol
unearthed the toll and jailed Voe Vole:
'Rot your soul without parole!'

This left Moe to raise tadpole
with no partner to console
in his lonely cubbyhole.

vole 3.
Climax

<u>*SORRY!*</u> Fox the climax *stole*,
giving plot a great big hole
hiding fate of vole and mole
and Po, superstar tadpole. [1]

---

[1] Po Orphan is the tadpole they adopted after Bulldog ate its mom in #67.

98. WAGTAIL, QUAIL, RAIL & NIGHTINGALE

Innocent Jailbirds

The trapped wagtail
and quail and rail
and nightingale
were sent to 'jail'
in Zoo travail
without timescale
or bail or mail.

Well bloody hell!

99. WIGEON & PIGEON

Is God a Duck?[1]

Does the wigeon
have religion?

'Not a smidgin!'
said the pigeon.

---

[1] Dr. Duck has volunteered to serve as Duck God if wigeon—*or anyone*—wants one.

100. YAKS et al. vs. DIAMONDBACKS

Zoogeography Lesson

Do yaks, hyrax,
old silverbacks,
muntjacs, addax
and rock macaques
all fear attacks
from diamondbacks?[1]

No, they relax
in different shacks.[2]

---

[1] Rattlesnake meant here. The diamondback terrapin is also Western Hemisphere but wouldn't likely be feared by any of these animals.
[2] Different Hemispheres actually.

101. ZIPHIUS WHALE & FRIENDS

Faster Mail

Ziphius, a smart beaked whale,
had a plan: 'It cannot fail!
Use my pigeon pal Fantail
like a plane to send my mail.
Air is faster than by snail.'

'Faster still,' said smarty quail,
'tell it to a tattletale!'

THE END

— signed Muse, countersigned Anil

News flash: <u>TARDY SHEEP RETURNS!</u>

Bo Peep's longest lost sheep has returned home, after these 101 were written. Her name is Sheep. She's a loner, the most strong willed of the flock, and hence got lost. She turned her anger against everyone and badmouths all 101 of Anil's and Muse's animals and rhymes here. She rammed this unauthorised AU in here regardless, calling it a book review, shouting "FREEDOM OF DEPRESS!" I was helpless. Although it is incorrect both politically and numerically, she threatened me if I didn't add it! — Ed.

101. SHEEP

The Misovanist

Little Bo's Sheep
thinks you're a creep,
you and your Jeep!
Not worth your keep.
Not worth a *bleep!*

Sheep thinks you're cheap,
not very deep,
don't try to reap,
don't ever leap,
act like a *heap*.

I heard her peep,
"You make me weep.
Please 'go to sleep'
before I sweep
you off a *steep!*"

How did she get to know you so well, reader? Did Anil tell on you? *(Me? No!)*